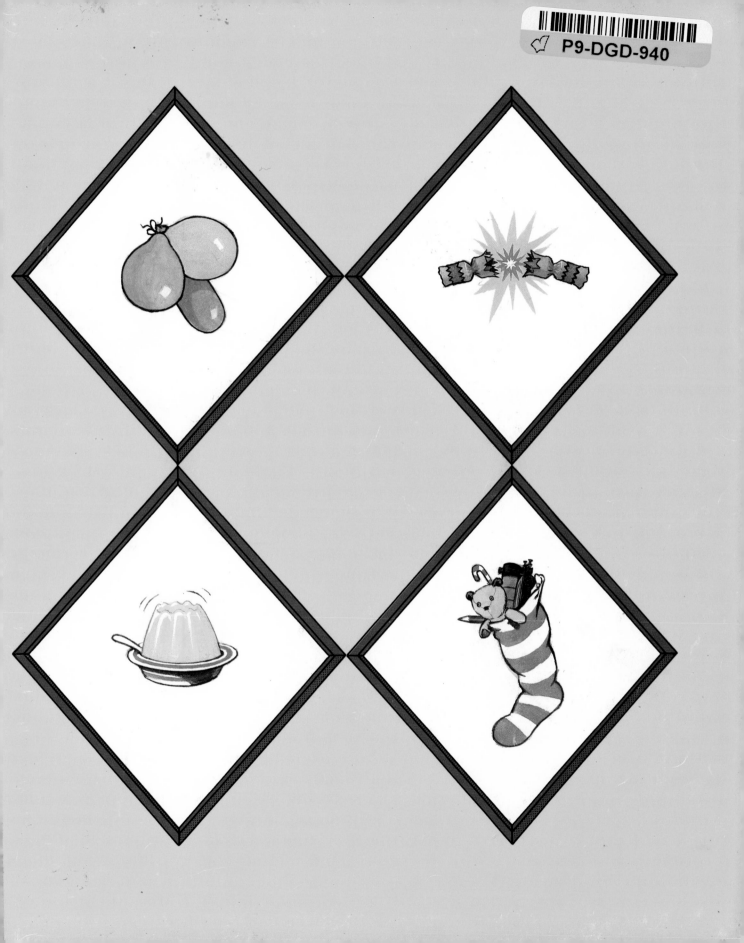

Library of Congress Cataloging-in-Publication Data

Moore, Clement Clarke, 1779-1863.
    The night before Christmas.

    Summary: A well-known poem about an important Christmas
Eve visitor.
    1. Santa Claus—Juvenile poetry. 2. Christmas—Juvenile
poetry. 3. Children's poetry, American.
[1. Santa Claus—Poetry. 2. Christmas—Poetry. 3. American
poetry. 4. Narrative poetry]
I. Stevenson, Peter, 1953-   ill. II. Title.
PS2429.M5N5 1985c   811'.2   85-17291
ISBN 0-918831-84-9
ISBN 0-918831-83-0 (lib. bdg.)

ISBN 0-918831-83-0 lib. bdg.
ISBN 0-918831-84-9 trade bdg.

North American edition first published in 1985 by
Gareth Stevens, Inc.
7221 West Green Tree Road
Milwaukee, Wisconsin 53223

First published in the United Kingdom by Hodder and Stoughton
Children's Books

Designer: Graham Marks

Typeset by Colony Pre-Press • Milwaukee, WI 53208

The Night Before Christmas

Words
Clement C. Moore

Pictures
Peter Stevenson

Gareth Stevens Publishing
Milwaukee

'Twas the night before Christmas, and
    all through the house
Not a creature was stirring, not even
    a mouse.
The stockings were hung by the chimney
    with care,
In hopes that St. Nicholas soon would
    be there.

The children were nestled all snug in
    their beds,
While visions of sugarplums danced in
    their heads.
And Mamma in her kerchief and I in
    my cap
Had just settled down for a long winter's
    nap,

When out on the lawn there arose such
    a clatter,
I sprang from my bed to see what was
    the matter.
Away to the window I flew like a
    flash,
Tore open the shutters, and threw up
    the sash.
The moon on the breast of the new-
    fallen snow
Gave a luster of midday to objects
    below,
When what to my wondering eyes should
    appear,
But a miniature sleigh and eight tiny
    reindeer,

With a little old driver, so lively and
    quick,
I knew in a moment it must be St.
    Nick.
More rapid than eagles his coursers
    they came,
And he whistled, and shouted, and
    called them by name:
"Now, Dasher! Now, Dancer! Now,
    Prancer and Vixen!
On, Comet! On, Cupid! On, Donder
    and Blitzen!
To the top of the porch! To the top of
    the wall!
Now dash away! Dash away! Dash
    away, all!"

As dry leaves that before the wild
    hurricane fly,
When they meet with an obstacle, mount
    to the sky,

So up to the housetops the coursers
    they flew
With the sleigh full of toys and St.
    Nicholas, too.

And then in a twinkling, I heard on the
    roof
The prancing and pawing of each little
    hoof.
As I drew in my head, and was turning
    around,
Down the chimney St. Nicholas came
    with a bound.

He was dressed all in fur from his head
to his foot,
And his clothes were all covered with
ashes and soot.
A bundle of toys he had flung on his
back,
And he looked like a peddler just opening
his pack.
His eyes, how they twinkled! His
dimples, how merry!
His cheeks were like roses, his nose
like a cherry!
His droll little mouth was drawn up
like a bow,
And the beard on his chin was as white
as the snow.

The stump of a pipe he held tight in
his teeth.
And the smoke, it encircled his head
like a wreath.
He had a broad face and a little round
belly
That shook, when he laughed, like a
bowl full of jelly.
He was chubby and plump, a right jolly
old elf,
And I laughed when I saw him, in spite
of myself.
A wink of his eye and a twist of his
head
Soon gave me to know I had nothing to
dread.

He spoke not a word, but went straight
    to his work,
And filled all the stockings; then turned
    with a jerk,
And laying his finger aside of his
    nose,
And giving a nod, up the chimney he
    rose.

He sprang to his sleigh, to his team
    gave a whistle,
And away they all flew like the down
    of a thistle.
But I heard him exclaim, as he drove
    out of sight,
"Happy Christmas to all, and to all a
    good night!"

Clement C. Moore

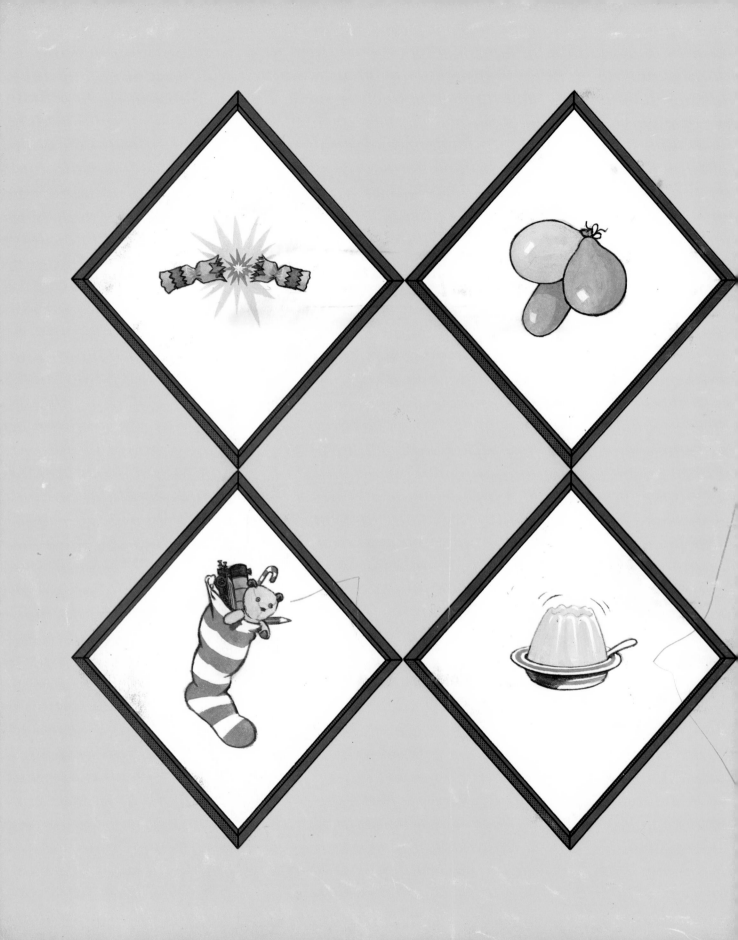